Inner Talk
for
Peace of
Mind

Inner Talk *for* Peace *of* Mind

Susan Jeffers, Ph.D.

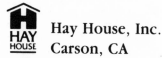

Hay House, Inc.
Carson, CA

INNER TALK FOR PEACE OF MIND
by Susan Jeffers, Ph.D.

Copyright © 1992 by Susan Jeffers, Ph.D.

The author of this book does not dispense medical advice nor prescribe the use of any technique as a form of treatment for physical or medical problems without the advice of a physician, either directly or indirectly. The intent of the author is only to offer information of a general nature to help you in your quest for mental fitness. In the event you use any of the information in this book for yourself, which is your constitutional right, the author and the publisher assume no responsibility for your actions.

Library of Congress Cataloging-in-Publication Data

Jeffers, Susan J.
    Inner talk for peace of mind / by Susan Jeffers.
      p.   cm.
    ISBN 1-56170-049-5 : $5.00 (tradepaper)
    1. Peace of mind—Problems, exercises, etc. 2. Affirmations.
3. Self-talk. I. Title.
BF637.P3J45   1992
152.4'6—dc20   92-15718
                                      CIP

Library of Congress Catalog Card No. 92-15718
ISBN: 1-56170-049-5

Internal design by David Butler
Typesetting by Freedmen's Organization, Los Angeles, CA 90004

92 93 94 95 96 97   10 9 8 7 6 5 4 3 2 1
First Printing, June 1992

Published and Distributed in the United States by:
Hay House, Inc.
P.O. Box 6204
Carson, CA 90749-6204

Printed in the United States of America
on Recycled Paper

DEDICATION

A Lullaby—
For the Fearful Child
That Lives Within Us All

PREFACE

We live in a very stressful world. And the child within us is often afraid. Yet, despite what is going on in our lives, it is possible to find the place within that is powerful and loving and knows there is nothing to fear. This is the place of the Higher Self.

I wrote *Inner Talk for Peace of Mind* to help you get in touch with the voice of your Higher Self. Most of us hear only the voice of doom and gloom. The negative chatter in our minds pulls us down and makes us feel vulnerable. It makes us want to control everyone and everything around us. The voice of our Higher Self, on the other hand, can soothe our fears by letting us know that we are safe and that we can handle anything that happens to us in life.

The comforting words that you are now going to read represent the power and love that live within us all. If you read them daily, they will ultimately replace the negativity in your mind. Remember that you do not have to believe these words for them to have a powerful effect. As you read their messages over and over again, they become automatic in your thinking and you will find yourself moving into a more peaceful state of mind.

When you can, say the words out loud. Intermittently, take a deep breath to allow the body to relax into their healing thoughts. Read *Inner Talk for Peace of Mind* just before you go to bed. Then, if you have the audiotape, let it lull you to sleep. When you hear, speak and read these soothing messages, the impact is enhanced. Carry the book with you throughout the day to be used when you feel stressed. Its message will help you feel centered and calm, will help you transcend petty upsets, and will help you find the best of who you are. In this way, you will always have a guide to your Higher Self . . . the place where all your Inner Peace lies.

From my Higher Self to yours,

Susan Jeffers

Inner Talk for *Peace* of Mind

• 🕊 •

I am now creating a feeling of peace within my body and within my mind. I take a deep breath and feel myself relax. From the top of my head to the tip of my toes . . .

I feel the tension melting away.

I feel the tension melting away.

I feel the tension melting away.

I take another deep breath and let the light from my Higher Self enter every cell of my being. I feel the warmth soothing all places of upset and stress.

I am bathed in healing light.

I am bathed in healing light.

I am bathed in healing light.

I take still another deep breath and relax into the arms of my Higher Self. I feel the safety and caring that my Soul radiates. I surrender to its magnificent strength. I am cradled with love and . . .

I am safe.

I am safe.

I am safe.

I now close the door to the past. I trust that whatever has happened in my life is a teaching for my highest good. I trust that I am finding the gift of wisdom from all my life experiences. I leave the darkness behind and I move forward into the flow of love and light.

I am filled with love and light.

I am filled with love and light.

I am filled with love and light.

I release my fears about tomorrow. I am on the right path. I am doing all that needs to be done. I am guided every step of the way. I relax. I am safe.

*My life is unfolding in a
perfect way.*

*My life is unfolding in a
perfect way.*

*My life is unfolding in a
perfect way.*

I rise above any matters that try to pull my attention away from all that's good in my life. I stop obsessing about anything that tries to take away my peace. I realize that what is truly important, above all else, is the love I give to myself and others.

What is important is the love.

What is important is the love.

What is important is the love.

I give up my need to control everything within and everything around me. I surrender to the Eternal Wisdom that fills my being. I listen carefully knowing that the answer always appears.

*I trust the Wisdom that
lies within.*

*I trust the Wisdom that
lies within.*

*I trust the Wisdom that
lies within.*

I let go of my worry about money. I release all thoughts of scarcity. There is always enough. I am capable of creating everything I need. I move into the light and see the huge expanse of possibility.

Life is an exciting adventure.

Life is an exciting adventure.

Life is an exciting adventure.

I let go of trying to control other people's lives. I trust that they, too, are learning exactly what they need to learn. I trust that they, too, walk the path toward their Higher Self . . . in their own way and in their own time.

*Life is happening perfectly . . .
for all of us.*

*Life is happening perfectly . . .
for all of us.*

*Life is happening perfectly . . .
for all of us.*

Although I live in a world of strife, I remain in the place of peace. I hold fast to the light of my Soul. I move my attention from my head to my heart. From this place I see things clearly. And from this place I know . . .

There is nothing to fear.

There is nothing to fear.

There is nothing to fear.

I trust that all is happening for my Highest Good, despite how it might appear. I trust that I am learning and growing from all life experiences. I let go of trying to control the outcome of all situations in my life.

I let go and I trust.

I let go and I trust.

I let go and I trust.

I trust that the perfect plan is unfolding. As the seeds blossom into a beautiful garden, so, too, my life is blossoming into overflowing abundance . . .

*I peacefully allow my life
to unfold.*

*I peacefully allow my life
to unfold.*

*I peacefully allow my life
to unfold.*

I trust myself. Within me is an endless source of energy that will handle all that needs to be handled. I push away all self-doubt and replace it with self-love. I constantly remind myself . . .

I am worthy of love.

I am worthy of love.

I am worthy of love.

I am finding a solution to all tasks set before me. I ask my Higher Self to show me the way and I relax knowing I have it within me to handle all that needs to be handled.

*I trust the miracle of my
Higher Self.*

*I trust the miracle of my
Higher Self.*

*I trust the miracle of my
Higher Self.*

I remind myself over and over again that, in all manner of things, I need not worry. I need not fret. I am doing everything that needs to be done . . . exactly when it needs to be done.

*One step at a time is enough
for me.*

*One step at a time is enough
for me.*

*One step at a time is enough
for me.*

I am whole . . . Body, Mind and Soul. I need no one else to complete me. I cut the cord that makes my survival dependent upon anyone or anything else. I know I am a powerful being.

I now claim my Inner Strength.

I now claim my Inner Strength.

I now claim my Inner Strength.

Each day I am learning. Each day I open the door wider . . . the door that leads me to my Higher Self. I have the Inner Strength to find my way.

I am finding my way.

I am finding my way.

I am finding my way.

I put aside all stressful thoughts and focus on the beauty of the now. The flowers, the sunsets, the caring, the touching of each other's lives. I open up to take in all the gifts that have been given me. Life is abundant. I trust that I am in loving hands and I know that . . .

All is well.

All is well.

All is well.

I am getting my priorities straight. What is most important is the love and warmth that I bring to the world. My life has meaning. My life has purpose. Every day I am learning more about becoming a loving person. The rest is unimportant. The rest is just part of the drama.

The only thing that matters is the Love.

The only thing that matters is the Love.

The only thing that matters is the Love.

I lighten up about life. Everything I do is perfect for my growth and self-discovery. I love my life and I am ready to receive all the gifts that are being offered me. I am deeply grateful for my many blessings. Life is truly grand.

I welcome it all.

I welcome it all.

I welcome it all.

I ease up on myself. I need not rush. I let go and allow the river to carry me to new adventures. I obey the laws of Eternal Rhythm. There is plenty of time for me to do everything I need to do. I constantly remind myself . . .

There is plenty of time.

There is plenty of time.

There is plenty of time.

I feel the light of my Higher Self as an everpresent beacon leading the way. I tune into the Wisdom of my Higher Self. I ignore any doubts inside my head.

*I am filled with peaceful
awareness.*

*I am filled with peaceful
awareness.*

*I am filled with peaceful
awareness.*

I am at peace. I imagine the warmth of the sun upon my face. I realize that my Higher Self is connected to a Universal Light that warms this world. I draw the Light into me and now gently send this Healing Light back into the world.

I am a source of Healing Light.

I am a source of Healing Light.

I am a source of Healing Light.

I am at peace. All the weights are now being lifted from my shoulders. I feel calm. I feel free. I let in the Loving Light of the Universe. I feel the warmth course throughout my body. I become the Light.

*I touch the beauty of
who I am.*

*I touch the beauty of
who I am.*

*I touch the beauty of
who I am.*

I pull up the Great Power that resides within me. The loving arms of my Inner Light envelope me and keep me safe. I feel nurtured. I let go of any need to control anything or anyone around me and I trust that no harm shall befall me.

I am at peace.

I am at peace.

I am at peace.

On the following pages, write those Inner Talk messages that touch you most powerfully at this moment in your life. Or, begin creating your own Inner Talk for Peace of Mind.

INNER TALK FOR PEACE OF MIND

INNER TALK FOR PEACE OF MIND

If you would like to receive a catalog of Hay House products, or information about future workshops, lectures, and events sponsored by the Louise L. Hay Educational Institute, please detach and mail this questionnaire.

We hope you receive value from *Inner Talk for Peace of Mind*. Please help us evaluate our distribution program by filling out this brief questionnaire. Upon receipt of this postcard, your catalog will be sent promptly.

NAME _____

ADDRESS _____

_____

I purchased this book from:

☐ Store _____

City _____

☐ Other (Catalog, Lecture, Workshop) _____

Specify _____

Occupation _____ Age _____